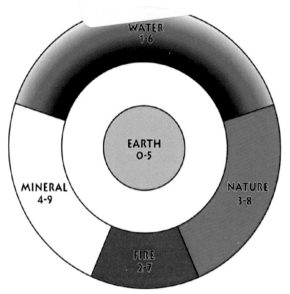

Africa To America

Dagara Cosmology Reference Guide

Web Content:

www.HealingDrummer.com

www.TobyChristensen.com

Email:
Toby@TobyChristensen.com

Africa to America

A reference guide to the Dagara Tribal Cosmology

Toby Christensen

This book is dedicated to my teacher, mentor and friend, Malidoma Some`.

Since 1991 I have been strongly influenced and inspired by this man and his teachings. The Dagara cosmology has changed my life in a way that has freed me from judgment, helped me embrace community and has been the driving inspiration for the development of "5 Element Sound Therapy" and my book "5 Pathways To Your Genius".

It has shown me how to bring my genius to the world and I am extremely grateful.

Acknowledgements

Most importantly I acknowledge and thank from the bottom of my heart, my friend and mentor Malidoma Some` who, two decades ago, saw in me the genius I was unable to see in myself and for investing an enormous amount of time, generosity and wisdom that has transformed my life and work.

Special thanks to Suzanne Lautz Singh for her years of support and prodding when I wanted to give up. She wouldn't let me!

Thanks to Mary Dusing who helped write the first draft and contributed much to the evolution of this project. Thanks to Robert Weir who lived with me for weeks in Hawaii editing and writing and creating the exiting format of this book when all I wanted to do was go to the beach.

Deep gratitude to Kathy Sampeck who has supported me and my work in many ways over the years, and to Carolyn Sampeck who while recovering from a lung transplant did all of the content editing of the final draft.

I thank my parents Corky and Arlene Christensen for always believing in me. Through thick and thin they have always supported. Good times and bad they have been solid and accepting.

Contents

Note From The Author

In 1998, I made my first trip to Africa. In my wake across the Atlantic, I left a flotsam of failed relationships, addictions, dead dreams, phenomenal financial success and catastrophic financial failure. At that time in my life I had come to the conclusion that my lot in life was to suffer. It seemed as though the "cosmic joke" was on me. I wasn't sure if it was karma from being such a terror in the world in my youth, from past lives, or whether there was some sort of ancestral curse. But it seemed to me, deep inside, every time I birthed a dream, every time I had a vision, every time I felt as though the success I desired was within my grasp, some force came from nowhere and suddenly snatched each and every possibility from my grasp the instant before I was able to get it within my hands. I felt as though just as I stepped through the doorway of fulfillment, the rug was pulled from beneath my feet and I tumbled backwards, to the ground, only to find myself back where I had been or even that I had lost what little ground I thought I had gained. I felt this way 24/7. It was the hardest time of my life.

In addition to the relational and financial disasters in my life, I had recently become homeless; everything I owned destroyed by fire just a short time before my trip to Africa. So that by the time I arrived in the heart of West Africa, I was an empty man – no sense of home, no identity, very few possessions, no purpose, and no material wealth. A being starving for something different, searching for answers to questions I didn't even know I had been asking, seeking a different way to pattern my life that could bring both the success and the happiness that had eluded me. It did not seem funny at the time, but as I look back, it does seem oddly funny. I was looking for answers to happiness, success, and accomplishment from a culture in West Africa that was rated the worst country economically on the planet. A culture that was completely absent of the comforts

I desired to bring into my life. Yet something called me…

And it was there in Africa, in the tiny country of Burkina Faso, that I encountered a way of being that helped me recognize what belonged in that void that haunted me every minute of every day, night, 24/7. It was there in Burkina that I reconnected with my purpose, my heart, and also "the drum". It is there in Africa that I stood in the heat of the day and watched people working diligently without technology. As they worked, sang, and danced always in the distance there was the sound of the drum. They always had smiles on their faces, always laughing, full of playfulness, and most noticeable was the respect they held for each other. At first it didn't seem possible that people could live in such an adversarial, hostile, uncomfortable, bleak environment and yet and be so content and happy. I couldn't quite wrap my mind around their way of being initially. But the more time I spent in their presence, the more I eventually came to understand the saying from an African wisdom keeper "the sound of the drum is the tuning of your soul".

Living in a village without running water or electricity is both a blessing and a curse. As is their custom, they welcomed me as one of their own. For two weeks, I ate what they ate, drummed with the tribal drummers, slept on the ground among the people, joked and cried with them and generally experienced first hand their spirituality, community and the teachings of the Dagara people. In so doing, they helped me re-birth my genius into the world again and for that gift I am forever blessed and eternally grateful. That word genius is a word that I heard from my Dagara mentor. You see, in the village, they say that each and every person is born a genius. Each one of us brings a dynamic gift into the world and it is the job of the village to acknowledge and support that genius that resides in each person. This philosophy, although foreign to me at the time, has become a foundation for my work and my life. Because my Dagara mentor saw the "genius" in me, this kept me alive and gave me the determination to persist, against all odds, and survive what became my "perfect storm".

My purpose in writing this book is to share my "perfect storm" and what I learned during my stay in Burkina Faso and my journey since then "there and back again" both physically and spiritually. I want to also share what I have learned in my twenty years of putting those Dagara teachings into practice personally and how I have adapted those teachings in my own ways and work to flow more easily with my Western mind without diminishing their power and effectiveness. These tools are deceptively simple, but at the same time phenomenally powerful and profound. These principles and truths will help you fill your own void, help support you and celebrate the discovery of your own genius. These tools will help you see that deep within yourself resides a power to help you express your own genius. The power in this magical place is the realization that you are intrinsically good and can choose to create life-affirming transformation and situations in your life.

Understanding Dagara cosmology has been of great value to me here in the West, as it will be for you too! I am more understanding, less judgmental, more compassionate and less combative. When you understand the energy that you carry intrinsically, based upon your elemental connection on the Dagara Cosmological Chart through both your birth year and ancestry, it becomes much easier to not take things personally and better understand ways of communicating. My sense of identity, home, and community became clearer as my genius flourished. More about this in the following pages!

For me the powerful connection to this ancient culture came through the drum and the therapeutic power of sound. As I observed these happy peaceful Dagara people and their community, I noticed right away that there was never an absence of rhythm and sound wherever they went.

This has become my life's work, bringing the therapeutic and healing power of the drum and music to the people of the West, to be utilized for transformation and empowerment, in connection to your life's purpose and to unleash your genius!

Blessings, Toby

INTRODUCTION:
How To Use This Book

This book is a users manual for life. It reveals clear direction for navigating life situations, how to discover aspects of yourself that you may not have realized and how to operate harmoniously in the world. It is a reference book that you might carry with you for a very long time. I anticipate that you will look at it someday with its tattered cover, dog-eared pages, highlighted sections, and maybe only then realize how this book transformed itself from an "interesting piece of reading material" into to a trusted good friend and companion.

This book contains the distillation of decades of study, thousands of sessions where this cosmology has been utilized to bring healing and restoration to people of all walks of life.

My intention is for this reference guide to help those of you who follow this path find a way to understand and effectively execute the power and healing that resides within this ancient tribal model.

CHAPTER ONE:

The Dagara Cosmology

The Dagara are an indigenous tribal people living in Sub-Saharan Africa divided between the countries of Burkina Faso and Ghana. Many villages seem virtually untouched by Western modernity. Electricity is a luxury not available to these people. Most have never seen running water from a faucet. That said, they are probably the happiest, and most content people I have ever seen. Without Western luxury they have a profound connection to the earth and nature, a deep shamanic tradition, and an active curiosity about the modern world. I remember a friend of mine who was raised in the village telling me the story about when their family came to the United States for the first time. Having never seen running water inside a house before, they would to get up very, very late in the night or early in the morning to sneak quietly into the kitchen where they would pounce upon the faucet and turn the knob on quickly to see if the "water genie" was still tending to this part of the house. They said the most fascinating thing that they had seen in their lifetime, at that point in their lives, was water literally pouring out of a piece of a metal pipe inside of a house.

Another obscure cultural aspect is that it is very common to see rituals and animal sacrifices being done in compounds throughout the village. For us Westerners it is very strange to think of having an animal in our presence for the purpose of sacrifice. It's like going back in time several thousand years. They go to the market and trade baskets of millet and corn for guinea hens and chickens, which are then used for ritual. The village members often consume the meat after ritual. These people are strongly connected to the spiritual significance of everything. Although they are among the poorest in the world financially, ironically, they are, some of the richest spiritually and arguably among the happiest that I have seen. It is rare that you meet a Dagara person in the marketplace or while walking along the street that you are not greeted with a big welcoming smile and a vigorous hello. The sense of community, and welcoming is extraordinary. It is not uncommon to hear the sound of women singing as they grind their millet under a Baobab tree, or hear the sound of drums echoing off in the distance. It was among these strangers that I was able to connect to my own genius again.

Sound and music are common medicine with the Dagara people. The traditional songs of healing utilize the voice, the drum and rhythm of the Balafone bring healing vibrations to rituals, village gatherings, and also aid when a community member has fallen ill or encountered an injury. This powerful sound healing is the medicine that opened a place deep inside me that has never closed, and continues to fuel the life that I live every day. Bringing this medicine back to the West has given me purpose in life. I will talk much more about this life purpose later.

Speaking of the medicine of sound, one of the best memories I have of my time in Africa is the laughter. The Dagara know how to laugh – at each other, at themselves, and their surroundings. Their oral tradition is centuries old and rich in a tradition passed down from grandfather to grandson, grandmother to granddaughter, father to son and mother to daughter. Their spirituality connects them to unseen realms, to each other and to all that is that surrounds them. Even before the world had an understanding of modern Quantum Theory, the Dagara, like most indigenous people, understood the interconnectedness of all things in the world. And it is from this worldview that this medicine of sound work has been derived.

Although they had no way to measure the activity of subatomic particles, they knew that through the application of sound, whether drumming or singing, that the energy in a person was somehow changed. Although they had no clinical studies, they knew that when the energies of the environment were rallied on behalf of a sick person, that person felt better, even got well. It is through this deep connection with the world around them and the "otherworldly" realms that the Dagara have established themselves as such powerful magical and healing people. Something else they have mastered so beautifully is the communication they have with these other realms. The Dagara literally have dialogue with the "Ancestors" as well as beings such as Kontumble and Genies. These other-worldly beings are a vital part of the Dagara cosmology.

Much like Chinese medicine, which we as Westerners are familiar with, the Dagara base their understanding of energy on a five-element system. I'll get into this in greater detail throughout the book and discuss the application of these elemental energies enhanced by drumming and sound for the purpose of healing. Although this view of energy and the world around them is predominant in their culture, a five-element structure is found in every aspect of the tribal person's life, not just in the process of ritual and healing.

The very structure of the tribe itself supports the five-element system. Every person in the village, based on their birth year are assigned tasks within the tribal community; they are sub-tribes [clans so to speak] within a tribe, if you will. These "clans" or sub-tribes hold certain responsibilities for the function and well-being of the overall tribal community. Each element has an intrinsic energy, color vibration, rhythmic vibration, and a numeric vibration. It is these vibrations and the overall energetic construct of the five-element medicine wheel that keeps the village intact, balanced, functional and thriving. The cosmological order of the elements is as such:

Fire - Fire is the first element that is called upon in a ritual or ceremony because it is the place where everything begins. It is the original element. It is the element they say was present at the beginning. Its primal nature is combustion, warmth, vision, and feeling. Fire resides in the south of the medicine wheel, and like all elements, it has a color vibration, numerical vibration, and rhythmic vibration. This element is about vision, dreaming, inspiration, feeling, and most of all and most importantly, it is directly connected to the Ancestors. And everything starts with the ancestors! Another thing about Fire is that it is the place to which everything will return. "Ashes to ashes…" Fire is associated with the underworld and as we walk upon the earth we are warmed by the heat of the Ancestors coming from the underworld beneath us. In the words of my mentor "fire opens the doorway to the spirit world and allows our psyche to commune with other life present, past and future. Fire is like a connecting rod, an open channel. In fact, fire is our psyche, the spirit part of us that knows what has always been. It is our ability to act, emote, and intuit. The person on fire is craving a connection."

Fire is the bridge between the seen and the unseen worlds. It is the place where dreams are given so that we can bring powerful spiritual energy from the world of the Ancestors into our world here. The color vibration of the fire element is red, the numerical values are two and seven.

People born in a fire year are the visionaries of the village. In our case we called them the dreamers, the innovators, those who can see into a situation beyond the obvious and get a vision for a new way of being. Fire people have a tendency to be very spontaneous and very excitable. But they are not necessarily very good at following through. Good motivators, not so good executors.

Water-Water is the element that comes second. It is the balancing element for fire. It is the element of healing, reconciliation, and emotion. Water is the element that gets the flow back into your life. The element of water quiets down that which is trapped in the crisis of combustion. In effect, water-cools the burning psyche. It stills restless consciousness and allows a person in turmoil to return to and settle into serenity. Water returns focus and coolness to an otherwise chaotic existence and seeks to calm, reconcile and balance the agitation of that which is in combustion. Water soothes emotional disorder and self-danger. When successful, water can restore and enhance life where there was once the threat of death; hence the connection between water and life. As it feeds the soul, water enhances one's life force energy. Water is the element that helps us slow down, cool down and allows us to notice things we often overlook as we run at high speed and helps reveal greater understanding. Water is eager to make everything work for the greatest good. The color vibrations for water are black and blue; it is a very interesting element that speaks to both the depth and complexity of this particular cosmology. Water is the only element with two color vibrations. You see, from the indigenous perspective, there are different types of healing that require different energies. The blue stands for conscious healing of issues that are in our awareness. Black water stands for deeper healing needs in need of other-than conscious healing. These conditions or issues may be deeply buried and, from a psychological point of view, may be repressed memories. Another aspect of the Dagara culture and cosmology that I embrace and love is that they see no need to re-traumatize an individual when the healing can be done on an "other than conscious level". If one can allow the energy of water to clear or flush their system, bring healing and reconciliation into their lives without the re-experience of the memories of terrible things that happened before in their lives, why not avoid the trauma? After all, if it sucked the first time, it stands to reason it will only suck again the second time. Sounds like a great concept to me. The element of water resides in the North of the medicine wheel, and its numerical vibrations are one and six.

People born in a water year are natural healers and they are the peacemakers of the tribe, of the world. They tend to be emotionally sensitive and are able to find the common ground in the midst of conflict. It is important for people born of this element to remember that it is fine to be able to see the emotional condition of a friend or colleague, but it is critically important that they differentiate between what energy belongs to them and what energy belongs to the other person.

Earth. The Earth element resides in the center of the medicine wheel and the color vibration is a golden yellow. First, the intrinsic energies of Earth are nurturing, abundance, welcoming, and home. It is the element about being at home here on the planet and being at home in the place that we live. Most importantly, Earth is the sense of being at home in your own heart and in your own skin. Earth symbolizes the mother and upon her lap we all find a home, nourishment, support, comfort and empowerment. As Malidoma Somé says, Earth gives us a sense of belonging. First, with being located in the center of the medicine wheel between fire and water, Earth represents survival and healing, unconditional love, and caring. Earth loves to give and she does give very abundantly! Earth is a great example of that which drew me to the Dagara culture initially because of its profound lack of judgment. The Earth loves and supports the wayward as well as the honest; both are allowed to walk upon her -- Earth. A person born in an Earth year is one who loves the world and finds comfort everywhere and anywhere. Scarcity is not a word in their vocabulary and they would give everything away before they ever taking anything for themselves. Generosity abounds when you are in the presence of an Earth person. The numeric values associated with Earth are zero and five. One thing that I so dearly love about Earth's rhythmic vibration is the meaning behind the beat. The Earth rhythm is comprised of a heartbeat, which represents the Great Mother's heartbeat. The heartbeat is always sending nurturing energy from the Great Mother; the heartbeat is always welcoming us home. The second part of the rhythm is two taps on the edge of the drum, what are referred to as "open tones". These two taps after the heartbeat represent our feet walking upon the Earth in gratitude. And so as the rhythm begins to flow, you have these two beautiful energies working together with each other -- the heartbeat sending nurturing and abundance and the two taps representing our feet walking upon the earth with gratitude. The nurturing mother welcoming us home while we come home with a sense of gratitude filling our hearts and blessing the great mother.

Earth people hold a place for community. They are able to create great abundance and when you arrive at an earth person's home, you are usually welcomed in grand fashion! They have a tendency to collect things; this is their need for abundance and their propensity towards making sure that they have ample supplies to provide whatever someone might need to feel welcome and at home.

Mineral–is the fourth element in this cosmology. Mineral resides in the West of the cosmological wheel with a color vibration of white. Mineral is about communication. The mineral people in the village are the storytellers -- they keep the history, the stories, for the tribe. Minerals make sure the elders' stories are passed down from generation to generation. The numerical vibrations of mineral are four and nine. Mineral people have a tendency to be detail oriented and are usually good with systems and organization. Minerals help people find the stories of their life's purpose and hold a very important place in the village. In the words of my mentor, "Mineral is the storage place of memory, the principle of creativity, resources, stories and symbols. It is the elemental energy that allows us to remember, to communicate with one another, to express our feelings, to receive messages from the Other World, and to remember our origins and purposes in life. These functions are what the human skeletal structure, made of mineral, is all about. In Dagara philosophy, our bones, not our brain, are the storage place of memory. In the village it is not uncommon to hear an elder say, "this is in our bones as it was in the bones of our ancestors." To the indigenous person, mineral is also the equivalent to stone. They see the bones of the Earth by the stones and rocks. As Dr. Some' states, "To know the true story of our earth including the story of ourselves, we must listen to the rocks." People born in mineral year often have quite the capacity to tell stories. Their memories are usually very good, but sometimes they can talk too much.

Nature. Nature is the energy of magic and transformation. The element of nature signifies the principal of change. Transformation, mutation, adjustment, and flexibility are all involved with the element of nature. Nature is about plants trees and the forest. Therefore Nature is all plants and landscapes and the animals and living things that reside there as well. Nature lies in the East of the medicine wheel directly across from mineral. Nature's color vibration is green. When dealing with the energy of nature we are working with an element that refuses to be boring or stagnant. Nature people are often called the "joking tribe" and are known for their constant game playing. They are famous for practical jokes. At times, nature people can be a bit disruptive, but once you realize the purpose of their joking, it is quite delightful to be around them. You see, the job of a nature person is to help those in the community and around them to find their "true nature". And so, what they have a tendency to do is joke and poke at feelings and/or aspects of ourselves we might label as "false self" from a psychological standpoint. And Nature people dig deep and are able to reveal the true nature of those around them and allow the person to activate and live their true power. One thing that I personally love about nature is the idea of magic and transformation. When I think of magic, I see energy free of restrictions, logic, and ordinary procedure. I visualize an energy completely free to be exactly "how it needs to be" to accommodate any particular situation. Something else about magic is that you never know how it will happen and it can be quite a surprise. So when we call upon the energy of nature and ask for its help, we do not have to know how it will happen. Another aspect of nature is transformation. Now there are a couple of primary ways to change. One very common way to change in the Western world is called "process". The other, often found in the indigenous world, is transformation. Process takes time and you can try process on a linear level. You start with one, then you go to two followed by three, four, etc. With transformation, you can start where you are and be transformed to where you want to be in the blink of an eye.

My favorite story about transformation happened when I was in Burkina Faso. We spent a day of ritual at the Great River. We were doing a very important ritual for two tribe members who had made a pledge that required an offering to the river. We set out on a journey with fourteen people, two goats and four chickens in a suburban. It was quite a sight. Those of you who have seen the old TV show "The Beverly Hillbillies" can just imagine what that packed out suburban looked like. We spent all day doing ritual and returned to the village for a night of drumming. We went to bed late and slept deep into the night; suddenly the village was disrupted by a loud scream. Something had happened and someone was in pain. We swiped the cobwebs from our eyes, headed into the center of the compound and there was a young man with blood dripping from his hand where a snake had bitten him. The manner in which it happened indicated ritual was necessary and so he was driven to a nearby shaman to determine what was needed to remedy the situation and learn the nature of this unusual circumstance. Before the young man was taken away I noticed a very deep cut between his thumb and forefinger on his left hand. This is where the snake had bitten him. We all went back to bed and while we slept, it was determined by the shaman that the spirit of the river had come to this young man in the shape of the snake and bit him to get his attention to let him know the ritual required an additional chicken. To remedy the situation, the shaman performed the ritual, and the boy was sent back to the village. I saw the boy several hours later and his hand was no longer bandaged. As I talked to him I noticed that there was not so much as a mark on his hand where several hours earlier there was a large wound. With great curiosity I addressed this issue to my mentor who looked at me as though I was the stupidest person on the planet. "Let me explain how things work here," he said. "He was bitten by the snake because a situation needed to be fixed, once it was fixed, there was no need for continued punishment. The wound was to get his attention; he paid attention and made the appropriate offering. It is all done". I insisted that the wound was human tissue and should take weeks to heal. My mentor leaned close to my ear, I could feel his warm breath against the side of my face as he said, "The boy does not know that". This is transformation! Wounded one minute healed the next. This situation also helped me see how many things I am attached to which I do not need to be attached. Because the boy was not aware of the time it took to heal a wound, from a Western perspective, he was able to heal in indigenous time…immediately! No process, just transformation.

My therapeutic practice and workshops are based upon the Dagara cosmology. Description of the five elements in the text above has a visual configuration, traditionally arranged in a circular pattern called a medicine or cosmological wheel (see Figure 1). It is a visual reminder of these elements -- Fire, Water, Earth, Mineral, and Nature. Each element is associated with certain properties that will be explained in greater detail, in the subsequent chapters. While I am going to present them individually, there is considerable overlap among them. For example Nature is viewed as the energy of change. But water in motion such as a tidal wave and the destructive aspect of Fire can also serve a similar purpose to promote change. So it is important to allow the elemental influence to connect to us individually in a very personal way. Many of us are drawn to a particular element which may represent an energy that will prove helpful in our daily life or with a particular issue we may be experiencing The ancestors call upon us to utilize the energies of the elements that are available for our healing and well-being. It is important to let go of any fundamental judgments for or against any particular element. We carry all the elements in our being. Our birth year element is only one factor. Our birth name also carries elemental energies and is another factor which I will explore further later in this book.

DAGARA COSMOLOGICAL WHEEL

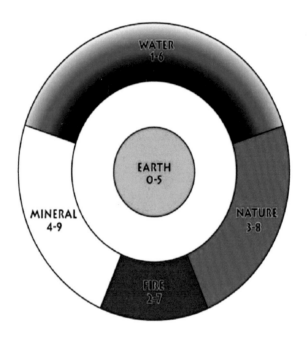

Figure 1

You may notice that some elements on the wheel are depicted as occupying more space than others. To the Dagara, the elements exist in balance within our world. The ideal ratios of the elements are 1:2 parts Fire/Mineral and also Fire/Nature. The ratio for Fire/Water is three to one. Earth being the center point, does not have a measurable relationship to the other elements. It is a profoundly important element in that it is the element that holds all the other elements together. Without Earth, Fire, Water, Mineral and Nature would not have a container. You and I would also be lacking a place of containment as well!

Most of us are strong in one or two of these elements, and perhaps a little less adept with the energies of the others. My goal with the use of therapeutic sound is to help you learn about the elemental energy that you do not hold naturally, or find the best ratio of elements, or you may need or want more of a certain element to give you a framework in which to hold all of these energies in balance within you as well. It is also imperative to remember that the importance of sound energy in this cosmology, and in particular with drumming, that instantaneous energetic balance can occur.

By working in conjunction with this five- element system, transformation can occur quickly and we can begin to see instantaneous changes in our lives. As we explore this system, we will start with Fire and then move on to Water, then to Earth, then Mineral and finally Nature.

This builds the proper energetic matrix to support your evolution into a place of your own power from which your greatness and genius can emerge and flourish.

The understanding of the Dagara is that everybody is born into the world for a specific reason – a purpose - to live out his or her own true "genius." From the time a child is conceived, the elders find ways to connect that child to their purpose for their "beingness" in this life. One viewpoint is that each baby that comes into the village is a reincarnated ancestor. Many of the rituals done on behalf of the child while it's still in the mother's womb have to do with finding out who is coming in and what gifts they will bring. The elders shepherd the journey with humor and love to help each child fulfill their unique reason for being present here in this world. This is common practice in many indigenous cultures, but we do not see this much in the western world. As a matter of fact, most children in the Dagara community are named to support their life's purpose. My friend and teacher (who I will introduce to you later in the book) named Malidoma, which in Dagara means *to befriend the enemy/stranger*. Through many harrowing life experiences, Malidoma has absolutely lived this mission. Imagine if your name meant *fantastic drummer* or *peacemaker* and your life's purpose was imprinted on you every time you heard your name. In the West we are commonly named after an ancestor, and often someone we don't even know. Our name may frequently be a part of family tradition as opposed to being looked at as a source of vital life force energy, gift, or purpose. In the west, a major challenge is that when a family begins to happen, the mother and father are frequently isolated. They have jobs, the two live in a house together by themselves, they may have some family support but it is not the same as having an entire village of support that you would see in an indigenous culture. So the western family does the best they can with what they have. In addition to connecting to the 5 elements that exist around us for our support, balance and well-being, there is a need that we, as westerners, have in our culture -- to create true community. And a need to support our lives and the lives of our children in a similar way the Dagara support the lives of each member of the village and the lives of their children in their culture and community.

The Dagara seem to think that there is enough room at the top for everyone. The people of the village have a wonderful philosophy that says, "If we all are profoundly successful at living our life purpose then we all benefit." It is amazing when we are supported in living our genius, not only do we thrive, but our communities thrive, our friends thrive, and the organizations that we involve ourselves with thrive. It seems to be critically important for us in the West to consider getting off the typical competitive journey, of what we call the "climb up the corporate ladder" and join together, to unify energy to make community stronger. While individual competitiveness seems to make community weaker, unification of energy only makes connection and community more cohesive. ·We could use the ladder of success in different ways such as widening the footholds or simply paying attention to who is climbing up the ladder beneath us and offer assistance and support. In this way, there is room for more than just one person to succeed and thrive. We can support the gifts that others bring so that we all may come into a greater place. If we do not feel we have the support of our local community, then we must look farther afield for support such as in a virtual community or other "support" groups. With today's communication technology, a community that is just right for you can be just a mouse click away. This initial community connection can grow as you do and connect you to new ideas, new people, and new places. There are so many virtual communities -- meet up groups, Facebook, twitter, and 1 million other organizations designed to bring people together. There is no reason one cannot connect with like-minded people. In my own work I have found it invaluable to connect throughout the world on a free service like Facebook. I have thousands "friends" on my personal site Toby Christensen and on my page entitled The Healing Drummer. These people and connections have helped me bring my work and healing to many parts of the world that I would never have reached had it not been for those means of connection and community. So as you begin to connect to community, do not forget about these tools that are available to you as you expand your own connections.

One thing I often hear from many people is that they are not able to see the goodness, or the genius, that resides within themselves. This is another reason why community is so important! Your community has the job of holding you in the space of your goodness until you can align yourself with this goodness fully and firmly. From this place of goodness you will experience your own genius – your gift for the world. As you begin to experience your genius, your altered thoughts and energies will begin to attract a tangible physical community to support you as well, in essence creating your own 'village'. You will have opportunities to also help those people around you align with their own genius as you hold your own space in the larger community in turn as well.

CHAPTER TWO:

Fire

Fire is a very powerful teacher. It is inspiring. It is motivating. Fire shines light into places that our eyes cannot see.

On the Dagara cosmological medicine "wheel" or circular "map" Fire is located in the position of South. It is associated with the color red. Red represents the fire that burns within us and the heat that radiates to us from the world of the ancestors. It's a color that draws the eye quickly and represents a portal to the spirit world. Red is often seen in West African art, clothing, and sacred items because it represents the presence of the ancestors. In the Dagara land of Burkina Faso, Africa, where Malidoma Somé calls home, everything is negotiated through the ancestors. Nothing happens without their approval, and things change speedily and in a helpful way when we consult with them about our needs.

In his Cowrie Shell Divination Manual in the section called "Element of Fire," Malidoma says: "Fire opens the doorway to the spirit world and allows our psyche to commune with other life present, past, and future. Fire is like a connecting rod, an open channel. In fact, fire is our psyche, the spirit part of us that knows what has always been. It is our ability to act, emote, and intuit. The person on fire is craving a connection."

A circle or a ring, of course, represents connection. In many cultures, a wedding ring symbolizes the marital connection between a husband and wife. Similarly, in the great circle or connection of life, Fire is not only the place of our origin but also the place to which everything returns. "Ashes to ashes and dust to dust" is a phrase used in

Western burial services to denote the full circle of birth, life, and death.

Fire People From a West African Point of View

In the Dagara cosmology, the Fire birth years are those ending in either a 2 or a 7. For example, if you were born in 1982 or 1987, you are a Fire person and inherently possess Fire energy and belong to the Fire Clan.

In the Dagara tradition, the Fire people are dreamers. They hold the dream for the village and the place of inspiration for all in the community. Fire people are passionate about their interests, visions, dreams, and easily sweep others along with them. They are quick to be inspired, quick to be bored, and quickly move on to engage in other inspirations. Fire people can be exhausting to be around because they are so full of energy and ideas. A little bit of Fire energy can go a long way and a lot of Fire energy can be difficult to contain -- which is also why the Fire section occupies a very small portion of the Dagara cosmological medicine wheel.

Fire is a complex and complicated energy. You cannot harness it, but you can dance with it. And just when you have it figured out, guess what, there it goes. Fire people can convince you that whatever scheme or dream they are hatching is the *best* thing ever, but they are not always dependable because generally they find many things that are the *best*.

Nevertheless, Fire people are great fun. Often, their dreams and inspirations are infectious and exactly what the world needs at the time it is needed.

Kindling Fire

To kindle our dreams and access the passion and intensity of Fire, we need to look at the things in life that inspire and impassion us. What are your dreams? If you could be whoever and whatever you want to be, who and what would you be? If you could do whatever you want to do, what would you do? What makes your heart sing? What kind of life makes you happy? What inspires you? What ignites *your* fire? What feeds the passion of your soul?

As you begin to see and embrace your dreams, you will find yourself in the path of Fire's profound beauty and transformative power. You will see resources of the universe align before you that are ready to come to your assistance. The beginning is simple. All you need do is light the spark, strike the match, and kindle the flame. Make the connection between Fire and passion. You will see your life bear fruit in ways beyond your dreams and imagination. This is the power of Fire.

Fire is this initial element on the Dagara Cosmological Wheel. The red stone, the Fire Stone, is the place where the diviners begin to read the map of your life in the present time. Fire has this primal power to grab wisps of possibility from the dream world, strands of hope from the imagination, glimpses of opportunity from the energy fields and then bring them forward and manifest dreams and possibilities into the realty of this physical world. Fire is *that* bridge.

Fire: Link to Our Ancestors

Fire connects us to the spirit world of our ancestors. The Dagara, and most other indigenous peoples, know that our ancestors are ever-present to help us in this life. The indigenous people know that the ancestors have a vested interest in our success; they are committed to giving help. But we *must* ask for help. Until we ask, they remain unable to assist. I don't know about you, but I sure can use all the help that is available. One of my African teachers once said, "You think the unemployment lines in this world are long, you should see the lines in the Ancestor world." With that high unemployment rate, the Ancestors sometimes have nothing to do, and they want to work on our behalf -- but we must give them a job to do! In other words, he was saying that too many of us do not reach out often enough or with enough desire to access the great Firepower of the ancestors.

And he is correct. In the West we are not taught to call upon our ancestors. So we don't. Thus, we leave them waiting in line, waiting for our request, waiting for us to give our permission for them to help. Since I learned the importance of asking the ancestors for help, I have not given my ancestors a moments rest! I invite them into my life often. And they deliver. I also invite any other ancestors who are looking for work. I have lots of projects!

Fire People – Personal Point of View

For those of you who don't know me, I'm a person who holds the Fire energy—quite a bit, actually. Fire energy has been present throughout my life, and it has made my life a very interesting, and challenging, adventure. Fire allowed me to burn my life to the ground and begin over in a completely different direction numerous times—as a musician, preacher, corporate sales executive, restaurateur, now drummer, shamanic practitioner, and a visionary. During those earlier years, I would rise to extreme heights and then burn through rapid mercurial decline into ashes in a cycle of about six to eight years. Each time, like the phoenix, I would rise from the ashes and begin again. This is one of the major challenges of being a Fire person. Yet, Fire has also provided the spark that ignited my work, my music, and even this book. Fire is the passion that allows me to help other people discover and nourish their own greatness, their genius.

This realization did not come to me readily or even easily. For the first thirty-some years of my life, I didn't have a clue that I was a Fire person. I didn't understand that Fire had been the common thread throughout all the changes and shifts in my life. I thought there was something innately wrong with me. What a sense of liberation when I realized that the destruction and reconstruction I experienced through Fire were instrumental to birthing *my genius*. And with that realization, I ignited with joy.

Let me explain about this realization, which led to my liberation. I want you to see how Fire has worked within me. Maybe Fire is working within you—or within someone you know. This may help you understand yourself and/or the Fire people around you.

In this book, we will actually go through in detail the nuances and characteristics of all of the elements on the Dagara Cosmology Wheel. It is through this understanding that we develop and will tap into the wisdom of the ancestors.

The element of Fire is very powerful. It will never burn out. The ancestors hold an endless supply! So, even if you walk away from your inspiration and your passion and submit to the mundane aspects of our ordinary world, as I did, you can return to your passion at any time and anywhere.

Here is the beautiful and interesting thing about the ancestors: They care so much about you they will not let you stray for long. As I denied my passion, left the music business and turned my back on the spiritual tradition that was so strong with my ancestors, there came a deep void in my life. I filled that void with alcohol and drugs. I used these vices as though they were destructive fires, they consumed me, and they burned me to a cinder. In effect, I was doing to myself what that fire did to my home and possessions. I was destroying myself and my life did in fact become a disaster.

Without boring you with an old story of despair, let me cut to the chase. I ended up in a one-bedroom apartment in Portland, Oregon. Though impoverished, I was desperately holding on to some trappings of success that remained from my life of perceived success: expensive clothes, a luxury car, and a lifestyle of feigned wealth. As I shared this story with you in the beginning of this chapter, this devastating event destroyed everything I had been attached to—all of my possessions, photographs, childhood mementos, everything— all had been incinerated, reduced to ashes. As I drove up to the smoldering remains, I realized that I now owned only the clothes that I was wearing and the car I was driving. I had lost everything and my world suddenly changed. It was at this point, while mourning that loss, that I met Malidoma Somé. Through this man, whom I've come to recognize as my spiritual brother, I reconnected to the drum. He saved my life, and I am forever grateful to him.

Within the ashes of the fire, I found my genius again. I began to understand that I was not those "things" that I had held on to so tightly for so long. I was creative, strong, and talented, smart, and compassionate -- someone better than I previously thought. I was so much more and was someone who could bring absolute contentment and fulfillment to myself and to others. I no longer felt the empty void that had haunted me for so long. Fire destroyed my possessions, reconnected me to the fire of my heart, and filled me with passion. Like the seed on the forest floor that needs, actually depends upon, the fire to heat and break open its seed casing, I was cracked open and germinated and released my genius in all its glory. I could now make my way into a new forest of possibilities. And these possibilities, unimaginable before, have come to manifest themselves beyond my wildest dreams.

And so may be your story. To connect to the energy of Fire, open your heart to what rocks your world. A friend once said, "Do what makes your heart sing and do nothing else." That has become my anthem.

CHAPTER THREE:

Water

"*People, especially people in crisis, are naturally attracted to water. Just the sight of a large body of water brings a feeling of quiet and peace, a feeling of home. Water resets a system gone dry. In this western culture the most crucial task requiring the reconciling energy of water may be the confrontation of overwhelming contradictory emotions carried by people*".
-*Malidoma Patrice Some´*

Water is the cooling agent in the Dagara cosmological wheel. It is the element that prevents combustion from happening in a time of crisis. It is the element that deals with emotion. It is the element of healing and reconciliation. It is the element that brings homeostasis.

The position of water on the cosmological wheel is in the North and is associated with the colors black and blue. The blue represents conscious healing. This is the still water that deals with issues that we know about, those issues or conditions that are present in our conscious mind. The black color represents the "other than conscious" issues. Black water deals with those areas of our life that you are not consciously aware of that need healing and reconciliation. In some cases we have an emotional response to something that does not make sense or for which we do not have a reference point. It is this black water, the deep-water, that finds its way into our psyche and brings forth healing without necessarily steering the conscious mind nor does it necessarily bring profound trauma back to the surface and into the conscious mind.

In his Cowrie Shell Divination Manual, Dr. Somé says, "to seek water is to seek vitality and blossoming that comes from successful self immersion. Water encourages a positive slowdown that permits one to notice things that are usually overlooked at high speed, and shows great understanding, and is eager to make things work for the greatest good. The water person thinks of community, relationship, love and harmony."

In almost every cosmological model, water is present. We see immersion in this element as a ritual, which takes place in every culture in various ways. The Hindus have their sacred bathing, as did the ancient Hebrews, and the Christians have the ritual of baptism. Of course the ritual of drinking water here in the West has become a multibillion-dollar business, a ritual in and of itself.

Water People From a West African Point of View

In the Dagara cosmology, the numbers associated with Water are those ending in a one or six. If you were born in 1971 or 1986, you know you are connected to the Water Clan. In the Dagara tradition, the water people are the healers and the mediators of conflict. Within the community, when there is a dispute of any kind, a water person is called upon to mediate or "referee" the situation. Water people are called upon because of their desire for peace and because of the need for peacefulness within the community in order for survival.

Water people are the ones who facilitate the "Grief Rituals" which are performed regularly in the village. Any time someone dies, there is a grief ritual. These water-oriented rituals are designed to allow people to express their emotions towards the individual who has abandoned this world and joined the ancestors. Often times what may start out as expression of grief about someone's death becomes an altogether different expression of collective grief around other issues within the village.

Regardless of where, when, or how the expression of grief starts, it is the release of the emotional energy that is important. The release of this emotional energy in a helpful way is critical for reconciliation and peace of both the individual and for the community -- the village.

Water people are often prone to excessive emotional sensitivity. They can walk into a room and are able to sense the emotion of the collective as well as the individuals present. A skilled water person can maneuver within a group in a way that helps bring cohesiveness and order. However, a less skilled water person can become overcome by the emotion that is present and take on the conflict within themselves which can have disastrous effects. And so it is important to maintain an appropriate and balanced relationship with this element as an ally.

Water People-- Personal Point of View

Water people in the West are often people who carry a lot of emotion. Often in the West because we do not have mentors who teach us how to work with our natural way of being, water people suffer tremendously from emotional disorders such as chronic depression, PTSD, and chronic misfortune. Their ability to tune into emotions, their own and those of others, can overload them and their sensory perception. Because water people can have difficulty differentiating or sep-arating between their own emotions and the emo-tions of others, there can sometimes be unwanted or uncomfortable results.

It is, therefore, critical for people who carry water energy to learn how to differentiate between the energy of others and their own. This awareness will make all the difference between a water per-son bringing healing to a situation or elevating the tension or emotional energy of that situation. Usually simple awareness is enough. But the ability to detect triggers and unintentional reac-tions is also important as well. Once this aware-ness is in place, the sensitive person can function well and in harmony with their gift and to mini-mize unwanted or uncomfortable reactions!

Another term we apply to water people is that they are often empaths. I have clients who come in and talk about how difficult their life is because they are so empathic and may say so as though this empathic nature is a torturous badge of honor in that they are so spiritual and sensitive. According to Merriam Webster, an empath has the capacity to recognize emotions experienced by another. And according to Dr. Judith Orloff [Emotional Freedom: Liberate Yourself From Negative Emotions and Transform Your Life, Three Rivers Press, 2011] *"empaths are highly sensitive, finely tuned instruments when it comes to emotions. They feel everything, sometimes to an extreme. The trademark of empaths is that they know where you're coming from. Some can do this without taking on people's feelings ... however, for better or worse, many can become angst-sucking sponges. As a subconscious defense, they may gain weight as a buffer ... or when thin, they're more vulnerable to negativity, a missing cause of overeating."*

Actually being empathetic can often be a sign of tremendous lack of power. It is wonderful to be sympathetic and understand how another person feels, but to take on that energy to the harm of yourself, is profoundly irresponsible. As a water person, it is important to look at what your own emotions are, own your feelings, and not the feelings of those around you. It is absolutely wonderful to be able to see and feel what's happening around you but extremely important for your own self to not to take energies and emotions of others onto or into yourself. This always has what I call "not helpful" consequences. In the West, we would greatly benefit, if not greatly need, training in our culture to teach people who hold this great gift of sensitivity and how to utilize that gift as a "gift and not as a curse."

Water people are the peacemakers. They are the ones who can find common ground in conflict. They are the ones who can see the "big picture." They are the ones who are comfortable when stepping in when conflict is present and bring peace to the situation at hand. As we see our world become more and more violent and our political parties becoming more deeply divided and separated, the job of the water people of our culture becomes even more difficult and, at the same time, evermore necessary.

It is important to remember that we all carry all of the elements within our being, regardless of the year we were born and to which clan we belong. It is just that our birth element is usually very significant and dominant in our personality, behavior, and in within the Dagara village our role within the community as peacemakers. The following exercise is a way to connect to the element of water and helpful way that can help bring healing and reconciliation into your life and create the flow towards connecting more purposefully to your life's purpose.

CHAPTER FOUR:

Earth

Earth is located in the center of the Dagara cosmological medicine wheel and is associated with the color yellow and the numbers 0 and 5. The Dagara affirm that any years ending in either 0 or 5 inherently hold the Earth energy and that the people born in these years hold a similar energy; for example if you were born in 1980 or 1995 you are of the Earth clan. In the village or community, it is the Earth people who hold the place of home, place of welcoming, and the place of abundance. An Earth person's home is often filled to the brim with "stuff" and scarcity is not a word, or even a concept, contained in their vocabulary. So Earth people always have something -- anything -- that they need or desire and they always have something that someone else might want, desire, or need. The Bonus – Earth people love to share. Something wonderful about people of the Earth clan is that they rarely shake hands -- they embrace you -- envelope you -- with a big welcoming, love-filled hug!

I am sure that you have all had the experience of going to a friend's home where you felt overwhelming comfort and welcoming, where you were well-fed, comforted, and loved as soon as you walked in. Or maybe that even describes your home? Chances are that this is a home created by a member of the Earth Clan. Within its walls there is an abundance of love and acceptance. The Earth Clan people embrace those in the community and create a space and a place where genius can be nurtured and discovered.

The element of Earth is found in the center of the medicine wheel where it serves as the foundation for all the other elements just as our planet Earth

[Mother Earth] is our home and provides the foundation to sustain our life – oxygen, ground, minerals, food, and water. Earth provides these things for its inhabitants in vast quantities, countless varieties and without expectations. This is one of the important lessons of Earth – that of abundance.

And Earth is also be one of the places where so many of us get stuck. Have you ever told yourself *I can't afford it* or *I don't have time* or *I can't help you, because then there won't be enough for me?* This is in direct opposition to Earth's outlook and its lessons of nurturing, abundance and sharing. And by giving voice to thoughts of poverty and scarcity we can draw towards us experiences and people that match that energy and thoughts – experiences of physical, spiritual or emotional dearth, scarcity, poverty, malnutrition and infertility.

So why do we tell ourselves things like that? Part of our cultural imprinting here in the West has been brilliantly created and then exploited by the advertisers of the world for almost everything and anything that you can imagine. Hundreds, if not thousands, of times each day in print ads, on TV, over the radio and on the Internet we are told we are NOT OK unless we have Prada shoes, Armani suits, Louis Vuitton luggage, Jimmy Choo shoes, or a BMW automobile. Anything other than those brands are not acceptable or their absence in our life means we are living a substandard existence. Worse yet, the message is that we are NOT OK as a human being if we do not possess or cannot afford those things. Trust me, you are beautiful and wonderful without possessing any of those things. It's perfectly okay to have those things, if you want them, but you do not NEED them to be valuable, important and whole.

A related aspect of Earth energy is that of having enough to share. We have been trained in a belief that there is a limited supply of everything and that we must get ours before it is all gone. In the movie Wall Street, Michael Douglas' character delivers a famous speech that illustrates this point exactly. *"Greed, for lack of a better word, is good. Greed is right. Greed works. Greed clarifies, cuts through, and captures the essence of the evolutionary spirit. Greed, in all of its forms, greed for life, for money, for love, knowledge has marked the upward surge of mankind."* This speech has become a rallying point for the Western belief system and actually has been for the last 100 years; it is the foundation of stock exchanges all over the world. And if you look around you, it is pretty clear that it is not working. It is time to try something different. It is time to stop hoarding just for the sake of "having". It is a time to take only as much as we need and to share what we have when we can. Time, love, money, service, goods, resources – there is enough for all of us, an infinite supply.

So, how do we change that poverty or hoarding consciousness if we have attracted it towards us? You can begin by looking for places in your life where Earth energy is working to provide you with abundance and then focus your attention there. Express gratitude for what you already have. Maybe you have a so-so job, but at the same time you also have an amazing family that supports you in all that you do. That is an example of Earth energy at work providing for you.

Acknowledge and be grateful for that which supports you. Ask that similar Earth energy to be extended into all parts of your life and begin to share what you DO have with those around you without fear of diminishing the supply of what you already have or that which you hoard in fear of losing it altogether. Something amazing can happen when you do this --suddenly you may find yourself on the receiving end -- you actually receive much more than what you gave away -- it just may not be about the "things themselves" but about what we do with these "things".

My teacher once told me that when he got down to his last $100 he would go to a good steak house have an opulent dinner and leave a big tip! This energy of abundance would remind his inner Earth energy to get the abundance flow going!!

If you are having a problem being grateful, I recommend a volunteer day at your local rescue mission or a trip to the burn unit or cancer ward of your local hospital. How about donating some time to work with disabled veterans. Volunteer to help people with learning or physical disabilities. Help the elders in the community at a nursing home or retirement center, Meals-on-Wheels, hospice; the list goes on and on. There is so much for which we can be grateful and so much we have that we can share.

I have lived in and now visit Park City, Utah often. It is a wonderful resort town with some of the best skiing in the world. I am privileged to work with athletes from the Ability Center who have overcome great adversity to become world-class athletes. Many are missing limbs, sight or hearing. They face a multitude of physical challenges. Yet their intention is to live their greatness regardless of the obstacles the world perceives for them. It is very easy to be grateful for my fully functioning body when I see what these wonderful people have been through. And I am inspired by the determination, kindness and generosity these men and women show to the community and around the world as they compete in their athletic events. We can find abundance in almost every life situation if we are able to open our eyes and hearts to what is around us.

Be grateful for what you DO have. Gratitude has a way of attracting more to us, abundance for which we are even more grateful, because we now have even more to share.

Another quality of the Earth element is that it represents home. Home, on several levels, whether it is here on Earth, in society, or within our bodies is a powerful place. Earth, home, is a powerful place from which to learn to be comfortable within our own skins.

Our body is another place that so many of us get stuck within the Earth element. Here in the West we view our bodies, our first home, as imperfect. There is little surprise in this, given the amount of media exposure to which we are continually exposed. Impossible Madison Avenue examples of airbrushed perky breasted women, being a size 0, or ripped bronzed lean male bodies are served up to us daily as the only acceptable ideal. Rarely, if ever, are we shown someone of actual size, with a disability, or someone older with wrinkles or grey hair. In other words, we rarely see someone who looks like us in advertising, in models, on TV, or in the movies. And sadly, over time with innumerable repetitions of this same iconic image, we begin to believe this and worse, that these advertising vampires are correct -- we are not okay the way we are in reality. In other words, we are not worthy unless we look like Angelina Jolie, Brad Pitt, Antonio Banderas, Arnold Schwarzenegger or have a GQ or Cosmopolitan worthy physique.

These illusionary beliefs are created and supported by a trillion-dollar advertising, cosmetics and cosmetic surgery industry that sells us the dream that we can be Angie or look like Arnold and then we will be forever happy with ourselves. Recently, for the first time ever the majority of young adults, when polled, said that given a choice of being pretty and stupid or plain and smart they would rather be pretty and stupid. The choice is not really that simple, we know this, but the results demonstrate that as a culture we have become ready to sacrifice our inner being in order to attain what we have been told we need by those who control this trillion-dollar advertising and marketing industry. And this is all based on a concept similar to Gordon Gekko's -- that unre-strained greed is good?

Those same advertising and entertainment imag-es are also a driving force behind eating disor-ders in young girls and increasingly occurring in young men. It has been shown recently that in countries without technology and mass market-ing, there is an almost zero incidence of eating disorders and a much broader acceptance of the diversity of body shape and size. In those same exact less technologically based countries five or ten years after the introduction of Western media's ideal, the incidence of eating disorders rises and approaches those of the West (1 in 3). I thought it interesting when I was in Africa, that it was quite the thing to be large. When someone is large, means you are prosperous and shows the world that you eat well. In Africa, being a size 0 means you are poor and cannot afford to eat well.

I have one word for the belief system of our vain western culture – It is time to re-evaluate our val-ues! The collapsed and narrow view of beauty that we hold right now is in direct opposition to what our Earth home shows us every day. Earth shows us where the surge of life across the African veldt is beautiful, where a loon rising over Boundary Waters is beautiful, where the rhythm of life on the streets of Manhattan is beautiful, where the fervor of the Marrakesh market is rife with rich smells and beauty, and where a full moon over the Himalayas is beautiful.

Spend a moment and connect into the rich and varied places of our/your home. Think of your favorite place. Find the unexpected beauty in home, Earth, any place that you find special. What does that feel like in your body when you remember this place? Energized? Calm? Bold? Teeming with life? Is this how you want to feel about yourself? You are no less amazing than that slice of Earth you just imagined. Try imagining that place every day. Connect to its smells; it's sounds, what it looks like, and what it feels like deep inside you. Connect to how you feel when you are there. In this way you connect to the Earth energy and bring it into your body where you can carry it around as you move throughout your day. And you can recharge this from time to time, as needed, whenever, wherever you want or need. This will begin to aid you as you let go of worn-out images of yourself, what you saw yourself lacking, and hoarding of all things no longer in alignment with Earth herself. This will align you with your power, greatness, and the abundance of all that you desire.

Dagara Earth Cosmology

Earth symbolizes the mother on whose lap everyone finds a home, nourishment, support, comfort, and empowerment. Earth, representing the principle of inclusion, is the ground upon which we identify ourselves and others. Earth gives us identity and a sense of belonging. Produced as the result of the collision between fire and water, earth represents survival and healing, unconditional love and caring. Earth loves to give and she gives love abundantly. Earth cares as much for the crooked as it does for the honest. Both the crooked and the honest are allowed to walk upon the earth. Earth's central position in the cosmological wheel stresses the importance of its visibility. Earth is the power to notice, to see and to thrill in being seen!

The Earth person is a lover of the world, of the earth. Unlike water, which seeks a way always towards one place, to the ocean, earth people find comfort everywhere, any way, and to give that comfort. Earth people, like Grandmothers, are people with a lot of energy and, as nurturers, want everybody to feel fed, content, respected and loved. Scarcity is not in their vocabulary! Making others feel good makes an earth person feel good. The earth person takes care of other people spiritually, materially and emotionally.

Earth People From a West African Point of View

From the West African point of view, Earth people are the members of the tribe that create abundance, welcoming, expansion and a sense of home. As stated before, scarcity is not in their vocabulary. They are big thinkers and know how to create bigness in everything that they do. As a matter of fact, many earth people have a very large physical frame! In West Africa, to be skinny is a sign of lacking. To be large is a sign of prosperity and abundance. Only the wealthy can afford enough food to be big, so contrary to Western protocol where women are supposed to be a size 2 or smaller, in West Africa the bigger you are, the more attractive you are!

Earth people in this cosmology are the greeters of visitors that come to the village. The person of the earth clan will rarely shake your hand, they will greet you with a big hug and immediately inquire as to what you might need to make you more comfortable. These people have the innate sense that the comfort of others comes before their own comfort and whatever they possess that can be of help to others is available for the taking. Earth people also have a natural propensity towards saving things. They never throw anything away -- just in case someone they might encounter might need what it is that they have.

If you want to learn about abundance, hang out with the earth people. They rarely question how things are going to happen, they simply intend and have an interesting ability to connect to the energy of creation. They understand that the earth is the provider of all things. They support an understanding that there is an infinite amount of everything therefore, everything and anything is possible and there is always more than enough for everyone to have all that they desire.

Earth People – Personal Point of View

Earth people in the West are people who know how to manifest. They are creators and have a natural ability to make things grow. Whether it is a community, a company, club, or sports team, Earth people have a natural propensity to create growth and creativity. Earth people have the ability to "magnetize" a community and they find it easy to rally people towards their cause on their behalf.

Earth people are about bigness and inclusiveness. You rarely see them arguing or fighting. Their goal is to bring people together. As I said earlier, earth people are more likely to greet you with a hug rather than a handshake. It is important for them to know how "you feel" more than it is how you present yourself in a superficial way.

Earth people are also collectors. Because they think in terms of providing for the community, they can often be labeled as hoarders or pack-rats. This label could not be further from the truth. People who hold a lot of earth energy feel it is their job to make sure that anyone they meet has everything they might need. Therefore, as the provider for the community it is important for them to have anything that may be needed. Depending on their elemental construct this may look like a well-organized variety store or a cata-strophic mess of junk everywhere! The important thing is to realize that their propensity to have stuff is about the need for abundance and care for the community, not about greed and materialism.

If you are constructing a corporate team it is im-portant to have at least one earth person on board. In the corporate world these people are so valu-able because they are able to draw a team togeth-er and help keep them unified. They also have the ability to spot areas of growth and expansion that may otherwise be missed. People with this energy are valuable resources to a community, to a company and any kind of social organization.

CHAPTER FIVE:

Mineral

One of the most surprising aspects of the Crystal world is its pervasiveness. All solid matter is made up of atomic particles arranged in some definite organized crystalline structure, called a "lattice." The crystal lattice structure, especially as it is found in minerals such as quartz, Beryl, diamond, etc., provides great stability of structure and regularity of flow of any electromagnetic energy that move through it. This is why silicon chips are used to provide memory and computers. It is also the reason quartz crystals can be incorporated into watches and clocks

to provide highly accurate measurements of time.
(From The Book Of Stones by Robert Simons and
Natasha Ahsian, page X X I paragraph 2, chap-
ter title why stones work: a theory)

According to the Dagara teachings, mineral is
the storage place of memory, the principle of
creativity, resources, stories and symbolism. It is
this elemental energy that allows us to remember, to communicate with one another, to express
our feelings, to receive messages from the Other
World, and remember our origins and purposes
in life. It pertains not only to the stones and crystals in the arts but to the skeletal structure of our
bodies, which is made of mineral.

In the words of Malidoma Somé, "in Dagara philosophy, our bones, not our brain, are the storage place of memory." In the village it is not
uncommon to hear an elder say "this is in our
bones as it was in the bones of our ancestors"
and to the indigenous person, mineral is also the
equivalent to stone. As the Dagara say, the bones
of the Earth are the stones and rocks that we see.
To know the true story of our earth, including the

story of ourselves, we must listen to the rocks."
(From a lecture on Dagara culture, May of 2011,
Washington DC)

Mineral is a very interesting energy in this ancient cosmology. It is about memory from past time, present time, memory from ancient times, and re-membering how to live our life purpose. It is an element that is bi-directional. On one hand, it is the element that holds the ancient knowledge from which we can extract to help us in our current re-al-time lives. On the other hand, Mineral can be a storage facility for information that we possess that is not necessarily helpful for us to hold and contain. The Dagara people say that the answer to every question resides within the minerals.

On the circular "map" -- the Dagara cosmologi-cal medicine wheel, mineral is located in the po-sition of the West and is associated with the color white. If the year of your birth ends with a 4 or a 9, you are a Mineral person. It is the elemental energy that allows us to remember, to commu-nicate with one another and to express our feel-ings as well as receive messages from the Other

World. These ancient people say that the bones of the Earth or the stones and crystals contain the history of the earth. The Dagara say that to know the true story of our earth, including the story of ourselves, we must listen to the rocks.

One of the primary information gathering tools of the Dagara people is a form of divination using cowry shells and stones. Because cowry shells and stones are both products of the Mineral element, information is stored in each shell and each stone that can reveal answers to the person receiving the divination. Many times during this ceremony, divination, information is revealed that would lead one on a new path of purpose and fulfillment. Other times information comes from the Mineral element that directs one to avoid problematic situations in their life, or to know who their partner is to be, or what path to take in life when there is an important decision to be made. The diviner relies on the wisdom of the Mineral Element to show this information.

Mineral People From a West African Point of View

In the Dagara cosmology, the Mineral years are those ending in either 4 or 9. People born in those years inherently possess Mineral energy and belong to that clan. They are the keepers of the stories, the storytellers, the teachers, and the detailed organizers! Because accuracy is very important to a Mineral person, one living in alignment with this element will be very organized, systematic, and have a very good memory!

This ancient tribe in West Africa has no written language. All communication of history is communicated via oral tradition, as it is in many indigenous cultures. Those tracking this history must be very accurate so that the ancestors and their actions, stories and wisdom are not forgotten. It is also important because the tribe relies critically on rituals and that these rituals are translated in a way that they are done with accuracy so the intended result may occur.

In our Western world of technology, computers and massive hard drives, and translating computer programs the thought of not being able to remember seems impossible. We often give our power to the machines, trusting that they will remember the details so we don't have to. This is all fine until we have a hard drive failure!

Mineral Creating Change

The element of Mineral is, in a sense, paradoxical. On the one hand, it is very stable, systematic, and organized. On the other hand, it can work powerfully as an agent for disruption, shifting, and change. There is a principle taught in Qui Gong that says, where the mind goes, Chi energy flows. This is very much a statement that connects powerfully to the Mineral, the element of which we are speaking. The stories that our minds repeat and continue to focus influence the direction of our energies and actions and can so subtly change one's path's direction -- for good or bad. This can be expressed in our words, posture, actions, and the results that we see expressed and materialized in our lives.

Let's talk about posture for a moment. If the stories of our lives and our ancestry are stored in our bones, then by observing our posture we could very distinctly see which information, or stories we hold, and those upon which we are focused. When you see someone standing with their shoulders slumped forward, head moving down, back slumped forward, this expresses an image of downtrodden, depressed, or low energy. When someone stands straight and tall, head held high, back straight, you see someone who is confident, directed, and focused. Often, when working with a new client I can tell, before they even speak those stories what they are going to tell me simply by the way they walk into the room. I can see from the way they sit if they are confident or fearful. I can tell by the way they move whether their intention is clear or scattered.

It is very common for those who come in with their head down, that they slump into the chair and begin to tell stories of pain, sorrow, and demoralization. This is the posture of "the victim". People who are victimized do not look into the eyes of those around them, they do not stand tall, for they have been beaten down and have adopted the story of defeat. When this posture is encountered, it is very important to help this person reframe their stories so that they can eliminate "the victim consciousness" and connect to the hope and possibility of regaining power and confidence. Regaining power often starts with realigning their bones. In other words, by simply working on one's posture, their structural framework, you can shift their attitude and the way they see themselves and their life almost instantaneously!

If the "stones" in our body are out of alignment, this can mean that the stories upon which we are focused are out of alignment with our life's purpose. By readjusting these stones, that is, realigning our bones and skeletal structure, we can change the flow of energy, which can then change our entire life! Often a client comes in, head held high, a quickened pace, and with an erect posture whether standing or sitting. These people come in with intention, purpose and are ready for energetic transformation! These people already have a fine-tuned, empowered life and are looking for even more!

If we look at nature, there are indications of how the element of Mineral brings changes. Often when the land gets out of balance, a landslide occurs. If you have ever seen a landslide, it is a remarkable and powerful shift in the construct of the land. I have witnessed boulders the size of small houses moving at incredible rates because the land was so out of balance that the weight of the minerals created a weakness in the infrastructure of the land and created a spontaneous and uncontrollable shift to bring balance to the environment. This condition also can occur in our body.

Our Western society is riddled with imbalance. People in our culture eat too much, drink too much, smoke too much, and live their lives for the most part, way out of balance. If we look at the economic system of both our government and individuals in our society, we see tremendous imbalance in our financial infrastructure. According to the American debt advisor, http://www.americandebtadvisor.com/questions/howmanyamericansareindebt.shtml posted on February 6, 2012, 80% of Americans are in debt. And that the people of the West are riddled with heart disease, diabetes, and many stress related maladies is not a great surprise.

It is this imbalance that creates the landslide of a decline in health, happiness and well-being in our culture. Although the United States and many European countries are seen as, or perceived as, the wealthiest countries on the planet, we are also on a collision course with destruction. It is the house of cards story that we have built that is about to come tumbling down. Depending on the stories that you identify with in your life, you can either join the masses living in the house of cards, or, you can begin to identify with another story that feeds your good health, happiness, and overwhelming delight in life! Regardless of your life situation at the moment, it can change!

In our lives, as in nature, when we get too out of balance, our foundation begins to shift and landslides can occur, usually with catastrophic effects on our health, relationships and virtually every aspect of our lives. An important acknowledgment here is also that catastrophic change is not necessarily bad. Nature shows us that often when a hillside comes tumbling down, the change in topography reveals something new that could not be seen in the environment's original condition. Same thing can occur in our lives. Quite often, those "things" and stories that we have held on far too tightly for far too long, as in our "sacred cows", become those very things that need to be released in order to reveal a new environment of our being -- ready for new transformation.

Mineral People From a Personal Point of View

In the Western world where we live separate from the magic of the untamed indigenous world, where we are not mentored by an elder, and are not taught to use our gifts and abilities, figuring out how to connect to this powerful Mineral element can be difficult and very confusing. People who carry the Mineral energy are often people perceived as bossy and know-it-all types. They usually have something to say about everything, and are very keen at correcting people when they speak in a manner that is not in agreement with the Mineral person. Minerals are usually very well organized, but they do not think they are. Mineral people are also always striving to learn new things. Minerals have very good memories and are very good at pointing out to others, what they should or should not do!

As you can imagine, this can be incredibly annoying, especially to a Fire person who is anything but structured and flies all over the place. When dealing with Mineral people, it is important that we understand these tendencies as intrinsic energies that are connected to their gifts. Otherwise, it is easy to go into a place of judgment and disharmony when associating with a Mineral person.

During my first trip to Africa I had a disharmonious encounter with a Mineral person. We had been working diligently on a new road for the village. It was hot, dusty, and I was very tired. I wanted some coffee, and some food! It also seemed to me that we were not utilizing our resources very well to accomplish our tasks. I began to make some suggestions on how we might be more efficient when a person came up to me, who will remain nameless, and said "As a Mineral person it is my responsibility to inform you that you are out of line and it is not your place to make suggestions!" I quickly informed him that it was my job as a fire person to kick his ass! If it were not for the intervention of my dear friend Malidoma, I probably would have done something I regretted. But to me, using the cosmology of these great people to justify this person's controlling nature seemed very disrespectful. This man was leveraging his personal control issues with the cosmology. Just because you are connected to the element of communication does not mean it is your job to be the boss of the world.

When we understand a person's tendencies, the way that they most naturally respond to situations, this makes it easier to have compassion and understanding. I know that my personal frenetic energy and fast-paced life can make it difficult for many people to participate in some of my activities. But, with a Mineral person, once we understand a potentially "bossy Mineral" person, having that understanding can make communicating and relating with that Mineral person easier, at least it has been for me anyways. After all, the Mineral person is responding in their "natural way", as a Mineral.

Understanding this cosmology has been of great value to me here in the West. I have become more understanding and much less judgmental. Today, I am more compassionate and less combative. Once you understand the energy that you or someone else carries "intrinsically", it becomes so much easier to not take things personally. On the upside, and a wonderful gift of Mineral people, is that they are awesome storytellers. They have the ability to see when a person is locked into a story that is not helpful, and to finding ways of identifying and reframing a perceived negative situation into a very positive transition and learning experience. When in alignment with their intrinsic gifts, Mineral people are also excellent teachers. They possess an ability to see things from many, multiple and simultaneous points of view and this can bring great wisdom to situations. Mineral people are very good at seeing the "big picture." They do not usually get entangled in the small limited viewpoint or feel "lost in a jungle" that can so easily distract many people. And certainly a big gift that mineral people have is the ability to identify one's life purpose and identify both necessary steps and possible pathways for one to connect with that life purpose.

CHAPTER SIX:
Nature

Nature signifies change.   It is plants and animals and landscapes.   It is situated in the east opposite minerals in the west.   It invites us to welcome change.   The magic we crave and our attraction to the supernatural are nature in their essence.   The tree, the plant, the landscape and the serpentine river zigzagging downhill on its way to the ocean, are all golden hieroglyphs capable of bringing understanding.   Elevated areas function like antennae, relaying and downloading information from far away.   Waterways take this information to the underworld.   Barren, flat landscapes emit a fast moving energy that is dangerous to isolated individuals. Only medicine men and women venture into wide-open places at night. In heavily forested areas the trees shelter human beings from the Other World. However at night tall trees emit a mysterious energy that may affect people's psyches as well as their bodies. That leaves the savannah as the ideal place for the Dagara. Sandwiched between two highly charged entities it is a natural refuge.

I have often wondered whether Puritans did not destroy witches, because of their fear of the power of change within them. Western history is full of persecution of nature. Progress seems to point to nature as its main enemy. Nature people trick us through humor into being real. A nature person is like a child, who sees life as a challenging play. Indigenous people embrace the wisdom of living close to nature and embracing its challenges. [Malidoma Some "Healing Wisdom of Africa"].

In a nutshell, the element of Nature can be boiled down to two important energies, Magic and

Transformation. These are very profound energies and are often misunderstood here in the Western world. For reasons I do not understand, it seems as though the "modern world" persecutes or destroys that which it cannot understand in a linear and logical way.

I searched many sources looking for definitions of magic and they all seem to center around one primary connection -- magic is supernatural! It is beyond our understanding. It is beyond logic. Although magic often does not collaborate with our reasoning, the effect of magic, without question, is acknowledged throughout our society, lives, and cultures.

I cannot tell you the number of times I have heard people tell stories of great despair, tragedy or even impending doom when suddenly a seemingly supernatural act occurred that delivered them from some brink of peril. This is an example of the power of magic. Call it your Guardian Angels, your guides, spirit allies, the hand of God.

The bottom line is that we have all experienced something at some point in our lives that has seemed like magic.

The Dagara people of West Africa are deeply connected to, and quite open to, living in a way that does not require western logical and linear thinking. Nature and magic are a regular and daily part of their lives. It is not unusual for them to be on at an outing and see an "Other Worldly" being materialize out of nowhere before their very eyes!

I will tell you this -- in the indigenous world one might lose their mind trying to "make logical sense" out of many things that occur, that you actually see! I saw things in the Dagara villages that were beyond my comprehension and totally blew my mind. I have no explanation about what or how these things happened other than they seemed to be by Other Worldly intervention!

Nature People From a West African Point of View

Nature people in the Dagara community are the tricksters. They are known as the "Joking Tribe". They are looked at as "a tribe within the tribe". They use humor, practical jokes, and tomfoolery to stir up the people of the tribe. In so doing, they encourage people to be their authentic self. They cut through the BS and protocol and get to simple and raw truth. The basic philosophy of the nature people is something like this:

People are reactive when they try to hide something or are not being truthful. When nature people encounter someone that is being reactive or are in a situation that requires finding the truth, the nature person will probe, poke, and stir the individual they are interrogating. They do so to see that person's responses. They do so in order to see if the person is telling the truth or being reactive. If the person is being reactive, the Nature person will continue to probe until they uncover the heart of the matter for the purpose of healing or to find a remedy to a conflict or the problematic situation.

Nature people can be extremely difficult to be around because of their tendency to stir things up. Because their mission and job in the village is to maintain truth and authenticity among the members of the tribe, they are constantly bantering with people. Nature people are constantly pushing buttons in order to maintain a place that exposes each person's "true nature".

Although this way of learning is very effective, it can also be very difficult and challenging. Many times I did not know for sure if I was being attacked or teased. It took many years of working with a Nature tribe person to come to the understanding of their teaching methods and, of course, to appreciate their respect for me in dealing with me the way that they would deal with another village member in Africa.

This is the way of nature. By poking, prodding, and bringing humor to a situation our true feelings, responses and reactions are brought to the surface. In that way, we can understand more clearly our authentic self and true nature. In order for the magic of nature to come through, we must be open. In order to transform, we must bring awareness to the parts of ourselves that require transformation. Nature brings us both -- it breaks us open and it brings forth transformation!

Nature: Friend or foe – Magic and transformation can be rough process

When working with the element of Nature it is important to remember the fundamental energies of this element. The two fundamental energies are magic and transformation. When I speak of magic, this is often an "alert" to those people with whom I'm working. Some think of a magician with a black hat and cane with a beautiful assistant on stage. Others may think about Merlin and the mysticism of the Middle Ages. Others may envision David Copperfield and other illusionists that trick people into seeing things. Magic, is a very, misunderstood and poorly defined energy in our Western culture.

From a Christian perspective, one of the greatest magicians who had ever lived is Jesus! He turned water into wine, healed people from catastrophic illness and maladies; cast out evil spirits and even he rose from the dead! How's that for magic!

There are many stories throughout history of prophets, sages, and holy people, who have performed miracles. These are people very connected to the energy of nature. In western mythology, when we hear about a miraculous event, it almost always takes place in nature. Many of the ancient sages of East India who are said to have been able to levitate, create objects out of thin air, and miraculously heal people are seen in cave drawings found in the mountains, away from the cities and deeply seated in nature. In the Bible, many of the miracles that Jesus performed happened in nature. The feeding of the 5000, stopping the wind when his followers were in a boat on rough waters and about to sink. And, of course, the crucifixion itself and most importantly the resurrection story -- all experienced in nature.

When I speak of magic in relationship to the Dagara cosmology, I speak of things that happen that do not necessarily follow a path of logic or linear reasoning. Another point about magic -- one person's magic is another person's ordinary life. I had my amazing camera story (Read 5 Pathways To Your Genius) along with many other equally magical stories when I was in Africa. But one of the funniest stories occurred on this side of the ocean when a friend of mine came from Burkina Faso to America and for the first time saw their first water faucet with running water. For the first week or so that they were in America, they used to get up in the middle of the night, sneak quietly into the kitchen, and turn the handle just to see if the magic water still came from this piece of metal. To them, that was magic!

The other aspect of the element Nature is transformation. We are going to talk about that in depth in the next section of the book but I'll just say for now, people associated with this cosmology learn to transform very quickly. In most cases, transformation is almost instantaneous whereas in the West process is a step-by-step system, which seems to take a great deal of time and requires a certain order. People who align themselves with the element all of Nature learn to transform in order to more efficiently operate in their lives, eradicate problematic conditions, and create opportunities!

Making Nature your Ally/Transformation vs process

According to Webster's dictionary, the definition of process is:

a (1) : a natural phenomenon marked by gradual changes that lead toward a particular result <the *process* of growth>

(2) : a continuing natural or biological activity or function <such life *processes* as breathing>

Nature People – Personal Point of View
In the definition of transform is:

a : to change in composition or structure

b : to change the outward form or appearance of

c : to change in character or condition : convert

You'll notice that process is about marked, gradual changes that lead toward a particular result where transformation is just about change. There is not necessarily a marked path or gradual change with transformation. I find that in a very systematic society in which we live in this western world, we rely predominantly on the process. When I am doing grief work, I often hear a client say "I'm going to have to go home and processes for a while." While this is absolutely fine there is another way. Grief, pain, disappointment, sadness, chronic misfortune, many maladies that afflict us in the Western world can easily be eliminated instantaneously through transformation. Transformation can be initiated by ritualistically connecting to the element of Nature.

Indigenous technology is such that one can jump from a problem directly to the result rather than wander through the streets of gradual and grueling regulation! Through direct connection to the element of Nature we can facilitate the release of problematic energy and immediately receive solution-oriented responses, whether through ritual, ceremony, or by magic!

One such case was a client who was diagnosed out of the blue, with stage IV breast cancer. Having attended several of my workshops, she was familiar with a particular ritual that allows one to release the energy they hold and transfer that energy into an object in nature. Once a person is satisfied that the energy has been adequately transferred they go into nature and dispose of the object that carries the unhelpful energy. After performing this ritual, in her case a few times, and this was a pretty big task, she was completely cleared of her condition.

I want to bring some clarity here. There is nothing wrong with process. I myself have undergone extensive psychotherapy that was definitely process oriented and it was helpful. I did however; find that as I engaged in these indigenous technologies, my issues transformed more quickly. And in the case of the bad habits, like patterns that were destructive where major changes were needed, these changes happened almost instantaneously when utilizing these ancient techniques.

I am very "instant gratification" oriented and quite impatient. So, for me, the faster things happen, the happier I am!

Claiming your magic

Claiming your magic also involves letting go of some things you thought to be true before. It is about accepting that, as soon as you release something, it does not have to return to you. There are many things in our lives that we carry that are not helpful. Wounds from our childhood, bad relationships, failed businesses, and things we have said or done for which we continue to carry shame. In process therapy, we talk about them over and over again. As a matter of fact, I realized after a year of therapy about my childhood that I had spent 365 days talking about the same things! And, unfortunately with no solution oriented results. I understood the problems, but they still remained there, with no solution in sight.

I'm a believer in "what you focus on, you feed." So, with this in mind, I began to focus more on solutions, not the problems. I found that as I focused on what I wanted to happen, or how I wanted my life to be, synchronicities began to occur magically that brought me to a place that I desired. It's kind of like filling a glass with fresh water, and letting the freshwater rinse out the impurities that were in the glass in the first place, rather than digging through each and every impurity that was in that glass and then filling the glass with fresh water. It is my experience, that when I dedicated more time to the problem, the problem stayed at the forefront and then continued to repeat itself. When I simply focused on the solution, transformation and solutions occurred "effortlessly and delightfully".

CHAPTER SEVEN:

Practical Application

The elements of the Dagara Cosmological wheel exist in harmony and balance with one another. So do each of us in society. Our work, family relationships and inter action with the world is a dance of balance and communication. Each of us is born into a natural propensity towards certain behavior based on our elemental birth year and the energy of the elements carried in our name. This natural energy we carry is the easiest and most natural way for us to function in the world. It is your genius factor. You inherently hold the energy of a combination of elements and work best when functioning within that comfort zone. It is your intrinsic rather than your trained behavior. None of the energies are inherently bad or good, although each certainly has both light and shadow attributes. For example water can be calming when in its still state, but destructive in the form of a tsunami wave. Fire can light our way out of darkness or provide warmth but also can be destructive when it burns out of control. While each element is helpful when used alone, they are often used in concert with one another as a "system" or even just paired in various combinations for specific purposes.

I have presented the elements individually for the sake of ease and clarity. However, they are most helpful when used in combination with each based on the situation of your life you are addressing. Sometimes you need Fire! Sometimes, you need inspiration and energy. And then there are times that the healing and peace of Water can bring reconciliation into your life. The Dagara have a great story about tears. To the Dagara, tears are meant to be shed. Tears are composed of water (healing and reconciliation) and salt which is the element of Mineral (communication and the holder of your stories). When you release tears, you bring healing (Water) and release a story (Mineral) that you no longer need to hold. This shedding of tears and stories can bring healing in the present and release of the past. It is a beautifully balanced and practical way the elements can work together in our lives.

As you begin to work with the elements, I hope that you will begin to create new rituals for yourself that involve one or more of the elements in creative and unexpected ways. If you create a new ritual or a unique healing experience unfolds, I encourage you to share your story of healing with me through my website at: www.healingdrummer.com

I truly believe that each and every person possesses intrinsic goodness. As I have learned from personal experiences, through my work, and the transformations I have seen in those I have assisted on their journey to self-healing, your "genius" will reveal to you the most supportive changes and transformation. And, when you follow the guidance of your own genius, your inner voice of wisdom, the community or communities in which you function will also be supported and enhanced. The intention of working with this cosmology is to allow the invocation of the energies of these elements to unlock your hidden potential, re-birth your genius, and for you to begin to live a life that dances to the rhythm of your heart, your being, and all that is you!

APPENDIX ONE:

Getting Assistance

Over the past 2 decades I have developed therapeutic methods based on the information in this book. This appendix provides you with the information to resources that can assist you on your journey. Please contact me if you have questions. My web and contact information are listed at the end of this section.

Shift It! Custom Soundtrack

Toby,

Re: Shift It. Okay, something that powerful should carry warning labels!! Forget surfing 50 footers, max wave first time out – by that I mean, at the limits of what the body could energetically take (and that was only part of the journey). Beyond anything I have ever experienced. 3000 years in 30 minutes. My new toy... my new portal to healing whatever needs tuning up...my new expansion into the next level of what is humanly possible in concert with All That Is. "Shift It!" is an understatement for this tool. Thank you Toby!! ~ Dr. Penny, Washington State

"The Silver Bullet" - The Silver Bullet- A straightforward solution containing extreme effectiveness, a device that creates a dynamic SHIFT towards your desired outcome and a quick resolution of issues that are holding you back!

Overview: With Shift It! we look at your long term and immediate needs. We look closely at your desired outcome and what is preventing it from coming to fruition. We assess the patterns that re-occur to sabotage your success and the places where you most naturally succeed. Following this assessment, we create a custom soundtrack to remedy prevailing difficulties and problematic patterns that affect your performance and productivity. This soundtrack will disrupt the unhelpful patterns and enhance patterns of success. It enhances open communication, creativity, productivity, reduction of stress and the necessary "shift" to support your desired results!

Objectives: To transform energy and actions that are not in alignment with your desired result and reconfigure them to eradicate negative patterns, situations and conditions. Get you functioning in a way that supports a sense of purpose, productivity, and personal power. Create an inspired mindset that promotes proactive actions towards your desired outcome.

Results: Accomplishment of your desired outcome. A better work environment, more energy, positive outlook on life, a sense of well-being, and improved self-esteem. You will also find that re-occurring disruptions are minimized and opportunities to create, motivate and produce flow more easily.

One On One – Personal Coaching

"My sessions with you were truly a phenomenal!
Truly an experience that has touched my very soul so profoundly".
~ Carol MS, Alexandria, VA

Need to know someone's got your back?
You know what you want but just can't seem to get there?

Overview: You get supported while achieving specific personal and professional goals. It is a one-on-one relationship that assists you in developing skills that will help you eradicate problematic behavior, habits and self sabotage, while supporting you in identifying how you want to move forward and what you want to move towards. This program will expose you to some valuable concepts such as "The Genius Factor", "Revolutionary Thinking", and "Creative Disruption". These concepts will help you see yourself in a new way, hope you eliminate old stagnant ideas and ways of thinking, and increase your creativity and personal power to reach your desired outcome in life!

Objectives: To get you moving forward in whatever way you want to move! To give you a clear view of where you want to go, a strategic plan to get there, and provide the tools and services you need to get there. Create a customized protocol unique to you and your needs of how to apply the tools for your greatest benefit. Provide you with the knowledge and skillets to pull you out of problematic behaviors as they arrive and learn to identify them before they have a negative impact on your life

Goals: Apply effective ways of managing your life, strengthen your personal dynamic and self-esteem, and eliminate unhelpful behaviors habits and patterns, replacing them with proactive behavior that moves you towards your desired goals and objectives in life. Create more fulfilling professional and personal relationships and increase your personal power and self-motivation. Most importantly the goal is to get you to your desired outcome with a sense of confidence, happiness and fulfillment!

Forecasting/Cowrie Shell Reading

As a psychotherapist, I can honestly say that you can be in therapy for years and not receive the deep and lasting transformation that comes from these forecasting sessions.
WOW!
~ Janet MS - Nashville, TN

Receive answers to your most challenging questions and situations
Forecasting of this nature is a systematic method with which to organize what appear to be disjointed or random facets of existence to provide insight into a problem or situation at hand.

Overview: What keeps you awake at night? What are your worries? Would you like to find the solutions? This method of forecasting is a doorway through which one can access the information of the soul, the place that holds infinite knowledge and wisdom and can reveal a perspective not otherwise accessible . A Cowrie Shell Reading from Toby provides a timeless view of the energy you currently carry, the direction of its flow. It offers a clear pathway for you to evade obstacles and achieve your dreams and aspirations.

Objective: To obtain accurate and helpful information to guide you in business, relationships, and life purpose, understand the condition and direction of your life and find insight and solutions you require to move towards your desired outcome.

Results: Problems get solved, questions get answered, you gain clarity, business gets better and relationships get healed. Accurate information and a plan of action changes your life quickly and leads you to your desired destination!

Genius Factor Assessment

Identifying an individual's strengths and highest potential characteristics is, identifying their Genius Factor. A Genius Factor Assessment reveals these characteristics and adds tremendous clarity to both the individual and how they fit into their team.

Contact me at the information below to schedule your genius factor assessment. This chart will get you started on understanding personal journey through this cosmology! I will help you with the rest.

Web information:
www.HealingDrummer.com
www.TobyChristensen.com
Email:
toby@TobyChristensen.com